On Huysmans' Tomb

Critical reviews of J.-K. Huysmans and
À Rebours, En Rade, and Là-Bas

Includes a critical review of *À Rebours*
by Jules Barbey d'Aurevilly

LÉON BLOY

Translated by Richard Robinson

Sunny Lou Publishing Company
Portland, Oregon, USA
http://www.sunnyloupublishing.com

1st Edition Revised & Corrected: December 18, 2021

Translation Copyright © 2021 Richard Robinson.
All rights reserved.

ISBN: 978-1-7354776-8-8

* * *

This translation from French is based on the "Literary Curiosities" edition of *Sur la tombe de Huysmans* printed on November 25, 1913, and published under the direction of M. A.-L. LAQUERRIÉRE, Paris.

The review by Barbey d'Aurevilly is from *L'Art Moderne*, August 17, 1884.

Table of Contents

On Huysmans' Tomb..5
   To Marguerite TERMIER..............................5
   Where is that Tomb?....................................6
Before Conversion..9
   The Sphinx's Reprisals................................9
   Huysmans and His Latest Book.................16
After Conversion..35
   The Incarnation of the Adverb....................35
   The Expiation of Jocrisse...........................52
Appendix..59
   Jules Barbey d'Aurevilly's Review of
     À Rebours 59

On Huysmans' Tomb

To Marguerite TERMIER

I offer these pages to you, my dear child, because you are gentle and good in my eyes.

When I wrote them, you hadn't yet entered into the world, and I myself had no other experience than that of poverty and many other torments.

If you should ever happen to suffer, one day, remember, as a Christian, the old writer who will have passed before you like a grievous shadow.

– *LÉON BLOY.*

November 1913.

Where is that Tomb?

Where is it then, that poor tomb?

Here it is six years after his death, the poor devil, and one might believe he has been buried for over a century now.

Those who wished to admire him, when he appeared among the living, are surprised today no longer to find an atom of his dust, and the sad books that he left behind no longer have their old power of boring even, they have become so indecipherable!

Having been his apostle, alas! having worked and suffered for so long a time to make him a Christian, the excessive mediocrity of his nature demanded that I should be paid immediately with the most glaring ingratitude, and that I should contemplate in him the most extraordinary abortion of Grace.

My disciple was acclaimed by our Catholics, and that says everything.

His bibelot and bric-a-brac religion appeared to them the result of a divine intimacy, and they accepted that the hopelessly thick Naturalist of *À vau-l'eau* should compare himself to the greatest Christian writers.

The pages that one is about to read mark two periods.

The first two were written before Huysmans' conversion, then when, full of hope and not foreseeing the atrocious disappointments he had in store for me, I caressed him with great zeal. The other two express the bitter disenchantment that followed.

People will not fail to accuse me of contradiction or inconstancy, which is entirely all the same to me. Someone came to ask me for these chapters, which have not been printed in book form until now, having been refused by the publisher Stock in his edition of *Belluaires et Porchers*,[1] and which might have some importance from the point of view of our literary history. Why would I not consent?

I will be reproached perhaps also for failing to show respect for the deceased. But "death," said Jules Vallès in the past, "is not an excuse."

> – *LÉON BLOY.*
>
> *Bourg-la-Reine, October 1913.*
>
> *Apparition of Saint Micheal on Mont TOMBE*

---

[1] *Belluaires et Porchers: Gladiators and Swineherds.*

Before Conversion

The Sphinx's Reprisals[2]

Œdipus really believed that he had vanquished it, the immortal monster! vanquished it forever! And for his victory the stupid Thebans made him king and a quasi god, that diviner with the *swollen feet*, that terrible blind man, a parricide and perpetrator of incest without knowing it!

For nearly thirty centuries, the human spirit sucks on that symbol, the most intact symbol that Greek antiquity has left us. In his irremediable fall from the luminous plateaus of Eden and in his successive posterior descents, the rational animal has always in this way held onto the idea of a central rebus, the unhoped-for solution to which would turn the subtle woodlice who discovered it into the rulers of the world.

If I could forget the horrible stupidity of the greater part of those who read me, and if the hands of a profaner had been granted to me, I would be less afraid to touch this redoubtable subject. Perhaps it is the most troubling thing I've ever met with... But rest

---

[2]The Sphinx's Reprisals: first published in the *Chat Noir* journal, no. 127, June 14, 1884, as "Les Repraisals du Sphinx." For Barbey d'Aurevilly's review on the same subject (*À rebours*), see the appendix.

assured, O my heart, no one will understand a thing. If I tell everything, penetrating minds will believe it is a sham or a simple smokescreen, and if I show some reserve the earnest will affirm that I am congenitally inclined to deplorable exaggeration.

"Does anyone wish to see Cleopatra in bed?" Dead and stinking Cleopatra? Has anyone read the latest novel by Huysmans? It is a morbid and desolate work whose title, *À Rebours*, gives no indication, unfortunately, of the dreadful depth of spiritualism and surprising energy of reprobation contained within it, in the name of a devastated Ideal.

* * *

Ah, well! Huysmans the Naturalist, the author of *The Vatard Sisters*, the collaborator of Zola and his repugnant clique in the *Soirées de Médan*, presents himself today as the solitary lamenter of defunct Christian spiritualism. That is infinitely unexpected, infinitely surprising, it is perhaps the most confounding thing one could imagine, but it is what it is – God knows with what intensity!

His book, a kind of terse[3] autobiography, in the form of an epitaph, exposes, on every page, a nothingness, the irreparable nothingness of all the stays by which the old psychic entity pretended to be propped up. Because "like a tidal wave, waves of human mediocrity will henceforth rise up into the sky

---

[3] terse: the word in French is *lapidaire*, which means terse but also lapidary. The extended "stone" metaphor (including epitaph) is lost in English.

and will engulf all refuge"; because, despite modern lies, there is no recomfort to be had for superior souls in the universal contemporary mire; because, finally, those miserable intelligences have lost the appalling resource even of a contemptuous and haughty pessimism, and "the *impossible* belief in a future life would be only pacifying," – what can be done? What the devil can be done about it? One cannot however re-sheath one's disgust and sink back down into the pig trough. That, at least, is as impossible as believing in a future life.

The Sphinx has returned, a thousand times more formidable. Its enigma no longer concerns man now but God, but no Œdipus presents himself to respond. Everything that nourished the infancy of peoples is insufficient and faded now. Theologies, philosophies, arts, and literatures are convinced of their impotence and insipidity. The old silique of hope squats in the rationalist's foot basin, and the delectable nutritive fruit absolutely refuses to appear.

The drapers of andouille, those fools of indefinite progress, and the trimmers of sideburns, those barbers of politics, do not seem fit for lavishing consolation, and their re-soled patter can have only one purely detersive action on the rare man untainted by gullibility. Any illusion one might have had is no longer tenable, one must either act like a pig or look straight into the face of God.

I do not see any other contemporary book that puts forward the alternative more definitively and more bleakly than that. There is not one page in it wherein one can rest or catch one's breath with any semblance of security. The author never offers you a seat to sit down on. In that kaleidoscopic parade of everything that can interest modern thought to some degree, everything is withered, ridiculed, vilified, and cursed by that misanthrope who does not accept that the ignoble man he sees everywhere is the true, final embodiment of man, and who desperately seeks a God. With the exception of Pascal, nobody before him has exhaled such penetrating lamentations.

But still, Pascal had an *ideal* God who was, after all, the invisible Samaritan of his distress, and who dressed his wounds. What's more, he belonged to a century in which something still flowed from the milk fountains of the Middle Ages, and he was ignorant of the exhaustion and parchedness of our own. He had the emollients of some intellectual diversions. He was a Jansenist and admired Montaigne at least. He sat down sometimes, with a modicum of good-naturedness, with that glaireous merchant of philosophical capotes.

But here it is quite different, we are at the extremity of everything. Catholicism does not suffice for that madman; because the *real* Eucharistic presence is not enough, he must have the SENSIBLE presence, although he does not say it outright, and although, perhaps, he does not realize it. It is the strange and new problem of superior beings at this so

Before Conversion

mysteriously exceptional end of the century.[4] No one wants a God that is hidden anymore. One begins to wish for a Christ that can be seen with one's own two eyes, radiant, fulgurant, terrifying, *incontestable*. Some say that the men who lived in Jerusalem or in Galilee, in the first years of the Christian era, were able to see Him whom Christians worship and whom the Catholic Church calls God made man and the Father of the poor; that for them it was doubtless easier to believe in him and that the countless multitude of others who have come later, borne on the slope of the centuries, jolted in the muddy ruts of history, crushed by all the extensive homicides of philosophy or scandal, must have had infinitely more merit to be able to surrender their heart and their reason.

All the books that have an atom of power or generosity in them have been saying the same thing for half a century now. They say it in one fashion or another, often even without realizing it, for it is a very deep shaking of the earth, as if something huge and extraordinary was approaching finally.

Never, in fact, have human theories sounded so hollow; never have the formulas of art been more exasperated and more vain; never has religious feeling suffered so prodigious a failure; never have the rich been more egotistical, more naively cruel, and the poor more fiercely impatient; never, finally, has a less tenable earth and a more demoniacal humanity

---

[4]Original footnote: Written in 1884. I was, then, still young and that is obvious, especially given I mention Pascal twenty lines earlier. – L.B.

been prepared by war or by the sordid traffic of all thinking beings' faculties.

* * *

There you have it, in all honesty, what emanates from Huysmans' surprising book, that erstwhile Naturalist, now spiritualist to the highest ambitious degree of mysticism,[5] who distances himself as far from the villainous Zola as if all interplanetary spaces had suddenly come between them. Read the haughty and dismissive epigraph of his book if you don't believe me.

It happens even, this significative thing, that des Esseintes, the fictive and unique character of *À Rebours*, who is nothing but a literary stand-in for the author, makes himself into a hermit in order to escape the impure contact, and soiled promiscuities, of social life. Neither St. Paphnutius nor St. Anthony exterminate their flesh in solitude, oh! no. But he escapes the face of men, and he is anxious for a superior Essence, and it really is a proud down payment towards the hermetic profession.

Huysmans' literary form recalls those incredible orchids from India which make his des Esseintes dream so deeply, monstrous plants with unexpected exfoliations, with inconceivable floraisons, possessing a kind of quasi-animal organic life, obscene attitudes, or menacing colors, something like appetites, instincts, a will almost.

Its contained force, repressed violence, and

---

[5]Original footnote: "prattle" would be more accurate – L.B.

mysterious vitality is frightening. Huysmans piles ideas into a single word and commands an infinity of sensations that are crammed into the thin outer skin of a language despotically folded into the last exigencies of the most irreducible concision.[6] His mode of expression, always armed and exhibiting defiance, never suffers restraint, not even that of its mother Image, which it outrages with the vaguest desire of tyranny and which it drags behind itself continually, by the hair or by the feet, down the worm-eaten stairway of frightened Syntax.

After that, what difference does the multitude of contradictions make, or the errors that lurk, like abnormal vegetations, at the bottom of a book whence all the blue of an immense sky drains as if into the watery expanse of a cursed gulf? What difference does it make, for example, that the dreadful priggish pedant Schopenhauer should be considered almost the equal of the author of *The Imitation*; that Joseph de Maistre should be judged *boring and* EMPTY, by the most incomprehensible of repugnances, and ranked below that academic plumassier[7] M. de Falloux?

What difference does it make that those Jocrisses[8], demented like Mallarmé, should be wor-

---

[6]Original footnote: What else could one say about a writer of genius? – L.B.

[7]plumassier: a person that deals in or creates ornaments of plumes or feathers.

[8]Jocrisse: the name of a stock character in French comedy, a kind of buffoon, known for his naivety and clumsiness.

shipped in the desert by that Hebrew in full Exodus, while Barbey d'Aurevilly is claimed to be sadistic and a sacrilegious raver? That last idea is a leftover from the old Naturalistic habit of emptying cesspools, as practiced by M. Zola, whom the author just barely escaped, and not a single piece of crap of whom will remain soon, I hope, in his mind or on his talent.

A writer of so healthy a contempt that he was able to lift himself up, all on his own, to the point of a mystical conception of *joy out of time*, – in spite of the most stultifying of literary educations – and who, so convinced of his having scaled the Mystery, shows to this squalid contemporary society the rigid and terrifying bust of the eternal Sphinx! That's all I needed to see, before which everything else grows pale.

Huysmans and His Latest Book[9]

A superb occasion to blather presents itself unexpectedly. Let the smarmy multitudes be exhilarated! Huysmans' new book, *En Rade*, just come out.

That artist has been much dragged through the filth and shouted down royally since his debut. One still remembers the tempest of saliva and Procellariiforme commicturition of all the press on the appear-

---

[9]Huysmans and His Latest Book: first published as "*J.-K. Huysmans et son dernier livre,*" May 8 and 15, 1887 in *L'Art Moderne*, a Belgian weekly. The article's preface to the May 8 article said this:

ance of *Martha* and *The Vatard Sisters*. The traditional archives of prudery and social pudicity, whose immaculate female chamberlain is the newspaper critic, were, in those days, emptied of their treasures; and the need to vituperate that novelist was so copious, that the key of the sacred chancelleries of indignation, which was turning verdigris previously in the back pocket of their functionaries, was thrown into the scrap heap. It was a fluvial outflowing of pudibund humors, an eruption of moral pus, an exanthematic evacuation of the whitish fluids of virtue!

The aquatic purity of the serialized installment was felt threatened in its most intimate glue by that independent moralist who had no fear of hitching up the skirts of souls and visiting their hearts using the speculum of the most imperturbable analysis.

And then Huysmans had the rotten luck of being a writer; he had that ineligible defect that must be unanimously reproved in the opinion of all obediences to public boorishness, while waiting for a just law to condemn it finally with some infamous punishment.

"We offer to our readers the first installment of an article by Léon Bloy, the extraordinary writer who continues in the tradition, at an extremely high pitch, and with a disconcerting originality, of the violent art of the bitterest of polemicists: Proudhon, Veuillot, Rochefort, Vallès. After his first works, pitiless for some among his contemporaries in the press and Parisian literature, he was placed under the damper, the most disciplined and coordinated conspiration of silence that has ever been seen. We are honored to offer in *l'Art Moderne* hospitality to this great artist with the poignardesque quill. Even if one cannot accept all his executions, one has to admire in him one of the most surprising literary phenomena of these times."

Everyone knows, however, that every veritable writer is radically incapable of producing a congruent philosophy. Criticism of art, psychology, moral or natural sciences, are all off limits to that clumsy oaf of the azure. The oracular importance universally conferred on appalling prigs, such as Prévost-Paradol or M. Renan, is conclusive enough, it seems; and the voltaic glory of that recent schoolboy nicknamed the "Psychologist," who discovered how never to write, by chance it would seem, is a sufficient counterproof of the saying by Flaubert, who died of indigence, that "this century has a horror of the written page." The greatest thinker on earth – supposing that such a monster could be born viable with a single head – would ruin and fricassee himself forever if he ever thought, just once, to try and write with eloquence. Such is the ineluctable and fateful norm!

* * *

The insuccess of Huysmans' latest novel is then assured, – royally. The author's pessimism must have prepared him for it, and the man of *À Rebours* is, without a doubt, invulnerable to all the juvenile hope of a literary justice discerned by the contemporaries of fat old Sarcey. He finds satisfaction happily in writing for the intangible pinch of artists whom the Republican ammonia has not yet suffocated. It is sufficient to read two pages from *En Rade* for the evidence of that opinion to leap out at you. Never has someone gone so far into the disgust of life, into the vomiting of his *brothers*, and, at the same time, never has so total a satiety of the human farce been expressed in so glacial an irony!

À Rebours has, beyond a shadow of doubt, been surpassed. The new work is not only even more bitter still, more desolately negating of any terrestrial joy, the style itself has grown more refined, perfected, sublimed, to the point of resembling that frightening metal that checks the progress of loathsome viruses when it is in a fluid state, and which, solidified by an atrocious cooling, becomes a projectile capable, it is said, of piercing beams.[10]

But contemporary souls are upholstered with a thick fleece of stupidity impenetrable by any sort of ballistic of Art. Moreover, while admitting, for a moment, that the form and color of this surprising book could be accepted by such a public, there would still remain the ideas and feelings that no suggestion could make it endure. The intensity of a writer like Huysmans is, principally, in his contempt. That contempt, the most complete imaginable, has no need of any sort of special outlet, nor any crateriform gob, in order to express itself. The well-known author of *À Rebours* has not at all the ignivomitous allures of an imprecator, and the torrential flux of green bile is, in him, merely the literary illusion of some prickly vanity that, pacifically, he tapped into. Indisconcertible and frigid, he spews, emotionlessly, on various flowerbeds where the stinking flowers of the incomestible legumes of modern art blow, and there you have all that he will agree to, that contemner incapable of being excited by anything. But God knows how that suf-

---
[10] metal: mercury presumably.

fices!

Since the scandal of *The Vatard Sisters*, Huysmans is in full possession of a label that nothing can remove. His name has become synonymous with "pornography," just as the name of the signer of these pages is evocative of all scatological vocables. No remedy exists for that identical nonsense. One could exhaust the most celestial dictionaries to tell the story of the empyreum but the augural formula would not vary. At the end of a century that is so profoundly hypocritical, where the semblance of thought appears to have buried defunct thought, the most legitimate employ of certain words is an attempt that nobody pardons, and it lasts until the most deflowered of immemorial hussies recuperates her virginity, for just a moment, in order to grow indignant in her cesspool!

What one has wanted to designate by the poorly fashioned word "Naturalism," and which represents for the multitude something of a prytany of filth, is not, in the last analysis, but a recent effort of the human spirit towards a new art, definitively emancipated from the down-at-heel paradigms of tradition. It is an ideal negotiation, by the same title as Romanticism, which it replaced, where the essential and unique business is, before anything else, to have talent or not to have talent. That primordial question has never changed. What difference does the pointless qualificative of Naturalist make when it is a matter of a Romantic transported by his vocation, the solitary ideal of which is to embrace sensible reality as it has never been embraced before, to reflect, to repercuss, to transcribe in high relief the normal sensations or symbolic images of life, and which really has no need for the dictates of some school of art in order to be persuaded that all colors are necessary in the palette to the artist who wants to paint everything?

* * *

Huysmans' intellectual genesis is common to the majority of writers of his generation, more or less inferior to him. If one must at all costs ascribe to him a master, it is Flaubert, and more specifically, the hermetic Flaubert of *Sentimental Education*, which nobody reads. Flaubert and Goncourt for language, Baudelaire for decadent spiritualism, Schopenhauer for dark pessimism, such are the incontestable influences that determined this protagonist of contempt from the start. But Flaubert has predominated, and his tenacious obsession is visible, above all in *En Ménage*, a work that almost succeeded, by which Huysmans ended his first stage as an observer and novelist.

As for Zola, his contribution is imaginary and nil in that vocation of an artist so vastly separated from him, despite the illusory confraternity of their spirits. All that was needed was the critical indigence of the journals to suppose a close relationship of inspiration between that mighty boor – whose cerebral apparatus, capable, as in *Germinal*, of inscribing and exactly restituting the most colossal of exterior visions, manifests itself so destitute at the precise moment when he must express the hidden perturbations of the soul – and that delicate inventor, that quintessentializer of ideas and sensations, that aristocrat of analysis who embellishes his style with so torturous a psychology as to discourage a king's executioner!

When *À Rebours* came out, in 1884, the world of letters had so clearly understood that Huysmans had finally divested himself of the pedagogic reminiscences of his art education in order to enter upon certain originality, that that book determined a literary trend. The synoptic pessimism of des Esseintes appeared to many as a stopping place or as a refuge, and the agonizing future of that anchorite of analysis excited the emulation of a large group of dreamers that the vomitive vileness of the present pushed madly towards a mysticism of any sort. They found in it, doubtless, the philosophical mysticism of Schopenhauer and the optative dementia of that crucifying resignation, but with the comfort of a superior æsthetic unknown to that German and not the least viaticum of a very faint hope of return to Christian spirituality. It was a quite unexpected, quite strange, quite hazardous outcome, but in the end Huysmans' book, unhindered by any deceptions in life, gave the impression somewhat of that which another, even stranger, book has recently called the "blasphemy by love."

The attribution of pornography was not abrogated, for the lofty reasons already mentioned, but it became imperative to excommunicate completely all hackneyed expressions from that merciless iconoclast who with a scandalously wrought style ground down the ancient simulacra of art worshipped for the last three thousand years!

Before Conversion

* * *

En Rade does not appear to be a work called on to modify that reprobate's destiny. The pessimism of *À Rebours* has been solidified and consolidated. Having supererogatorily documented, for three years, additional disgusts in a continuation of the same existence, the author, unable to surpass himself in an iterative exposé of our filthiness, decided to prune off des Esseintes' indistinct, crepuscular postulate towards a divine release.

No counterweight from now on to the deep despondency of souls. No pale brightness, no wan glimmer of the skies in the falling of that terrifying night at the end of ages! Never has hope been so positively dismissed. One gets to a point even of no longer being able to discern a dogmatic pessimism announced in some tumulary philosophical gospel; it is the final Nihilism that makes its way, quietly, unobtrusively, into the vestibule with no prior creaking of the hinges, while it makes its way into the antechamber without the gnashing of teeth, with velvet paws and closed lips, wearing the doleful mask of a sardonic dreamer. The tragic and penumbral Souvarine, in Zola's *Germinal*, is an exact physical portrait of Huysmans, whose deflowering literature – all the while supposing that its curiousness of style did not prevent it from being accepted – would surely become a greater social peril for the octogenarian century than the terrifying catastrophes incited by sectarian demoniacs!

"Alone, the worst comes." Such is, borrowed

from Schopenhauer, the philosophical watchword of that distressing spirit. One can, effortlessly, represent to oneself the effect on adolescent brains of that galley-slave mandate, uniformly placarded in all the gallies of intelligence, by the episcopal will of an incontestable artist. Does anyone want to know how Truth appeared to him in a nightmare?

"The woman was now seated on the edge of one of those towers of Saint-Sulpice; but what a woman! a sordid whore, who laughed in a dissolute and mocking fashion, a dirty rag coiffed with a bundle of shallots on the top of her head, her bangs on fire, runny eyes, with bags under them, no nasal root, her nose crushed at the end, her mouth ruined, with no teeth in front, caries in the back, barred like that of a clown, with two dabs of blood.

"She resembled, at one and the same time, a military camp prostitute and an upholsterer, and she sniggered, tapped her heel on the tower, made eyes at the sky, hung the beggar's pouch of her two old teats over the square below, the half-closed shutters of her paunch, the rough goatskin of her vast thighs, between which blossomed the dry tuft of an ignoble mattress varec... That abominable whore, – she was Truth.

"How sloppy and misshapen she was! And for all that, men continue to pass her around for so many centuries! In fact, what is so surprising? Is not Truth the great Slattern of the spirit, the great Slut of the soul?... Supernatural for some, earthy for others, she seeds conviction indifferently in the Mesopotamia of elevated souls and in the spiritual Sologne of idiots; she caressed each one of them, according to his temperament, according to his illusions and his manias, according to his age, offered herself to his concupiscence of certitude, in all postures, on all sides, one had only to choose."[11] [12]

There are three of them, nightmares, in that anormal novel, nightmares or dreams. The first, the evocation of a Biblical palace, refulgent with every Oriental gem and filled with the terrifying majesty of the solitary King, at whose feet all of a sudden a frail virgin appears, "aureoled by a halo of aromas," a flower of flesh, exquisite, melancholic by force of an almost superhuman beauty in whom the dreamer is pleased to verify as Esther in the presence of her old monarch, whose senile heart she alone will have the power to stir; later, a trip of exploration to the arid and luminous sierras of the Moon "in that indissoluble silence that volplanes, since eternity, under the immense darkness of an incomprehensible sky." That bizarre episode is an inconceivable literary tour de force, of a perversity of unprecedented language, but never has a more implacable will been seen that contravened the comminatory injunctions of the Infinite. One would seek in vain for something more disconcerting. Huysmans employs all his strength to discourage in himself a divine presentiment, and his lyri-

---

[11] Original footnote: *Ego sum Veritas*, said Jesus. Has Huysmans, having become a Christian, realized the enormity of his blasphemy? – L.B.

[12] The quote is from chapter X of *En Rade*.

cal pilgrimage on the silver fringe of that robe of constellations, that no plausible Lord God sweeps Space with, finishes by resembling the portentous defiance of some scaler of heaven! Finally, one of the last impressions of the book is the perfect incoherence and total delirium of the authentic nightmare from which arose the hideous allegory just cited.

That tumultuous intrusion of the most mysterious phenomena of sleep into a novel devoid of dramatic peripeteia, executed, moreover, with that rigorous probity of an artist who does not conform, for one second, to the sentimental exigencies of the reader, has particularly disconcerted the readership of *The Independent Review*, where that extraordinary work was published. Some have accused that novelty of madness, as if the novelist's art must still obey, as in the old days of Romanticism, the cliched methods of a mechanical fabulation. It is not difficult to presume, however, that the culminating, over-the-top æsthetician of *À Rebours*, vanquished by the incommutable destiny of unpopularity of every veritable artist, but inept at changing, has quite naturally chosen the unlimited estuary of his dreams to disgorge the inconfessable spirituality of his thought!...

* * *

In fact, that title, *En Rade*, is a lamentable untruth. There is no harbor at all, no shelter, no security of any sort. One dies of agony, disgust, and ennui in that crumbling chateau in Lourps, where one had hoped to find a refuge. One would do one hundred times better – to keep within the metaphor – taking to the open seas and risking all possible shipwrecks! One would at least have a fighting chance at being pushed towards some more hospitable haven.

If the soul of the author is complex – and it certainly! does not seem easy to find another author who is more so – the fiction of his book is, on the other hand, of a lineamental ingenuity. No one will ever be made to write a novel more devoid of any dramatic mechanism or scheme. It is the story, pure and simple, of a poor devil, a distinguished man, but feebly gifted in financial matters, who, ruined the day before by the judicious bankruptcy of a nimble banker, hopes for a bit of relief from his torments in a solitude in Brie where his wife's relatives, peasants whom she barely knows, have offered the hospitality of a pile of rubble to those cleaned-out Parisians whose distress they know nothing about.

It does not take Jacques Marles, the protagonist, long to discover the ignoble cupidity of his hosts who only lured him into their hovel with the hopes of swindling him in broad daylight, and, no less swift at sniffing out his penury, they soon no longer bother to try to hide their cannibalism of castaways.

From then on one sees the charming holiday of that unfortunate man devoured by disquietudes for the most immediate future, racked by his ill wife who does not forgive him his lack of foresight, forced to dispute at every instant his last resources with the sordid improbity of the entire countryside, sandbagged in an inhabitable and sinister kennel, that does not offer even the intellectual compensation of any archeological interest, oppressed by demential nocturnal hallucinations that appear to communicate with the inexplicable free passageways of that defunct chateau, reduced finally to taking flight in order to escape the raging horror of that harbor of malediction!

That's it, to be quite honest. One must acknowledge that one would need one hell of a genius for the scenic adaptation of such a poem! But what is much more important than the touched-up effects of the low serialized novel is the proliferating interest of observation that gallops rampant through those pages and the more or less plausible novelty of insights discovered in it.

Rustics have been the major focus of literature for the last fifty years, and those sordid brutes have come out on top. One has wished, all too often, that the external magnificence of nature should permeate them. One has even seen them, sometimes, very majestic under the sonorous foliage or the evening firmaments. The *Angelus* by the painter Millet will continue for a long time to inform sensible hearts of the religious humility of those resigned children of the earth. The old sentimental wench George Sand has certified them full of idyls while saturating them with her juice. With all his hullabaloo, Cladel has declared them epic, and his disciple Lemonnier has forbidden anyone to suppose them inferior to Polyphemus. How many others still, among writers, conscientious ones even, who have been unable to see in the peasant anything less than an associate of Nature, accompanied at least by its diffuse melancholy, when he was not at its same majesty! Only Balzac discerned the obtuse baseness of those unruly hypocrites. But that great analyst, adumbrated by syntheses, found himself overcome almost immediately, confiscated by a historical conception of the *Jacquerie*,[13] of the permanent and organized conspiration of the people of the countryside against the holders of the soil, and his peasants were cosmopolites in the manner of barbarians. They could be indifferently Tourangeaux or Languedocians.

With a view to escaping that hovering but inexact vision, refracted into infinite atmospheres, Huysmans wanted to billet his observation in a very special corner of France, very clearly designated by him. He lived the life of its peasants there, hour by hour, recording their gestures, their phrases, their physiognomies, without concern for any limitrophe peasantry, serenely assured of encountering – in the integral precision of his notes – the meridian of profound solidarity sought by abstractors of systems.

Will an equitable critic give that artist his just due, while recognizing that never before him have peasants been depicted in such illuminating and rigorous tonality? That is infinitely doubtful. Nevertheless, that is how it is, and sentimental theories, any more than the prejudices of schools, can do nothing about it. The veridical peasants of *En Rade* thrash about, bellow, guzzle in the manner of the Flemish people

---

[13]*Jacquerie*: the peasant revolt of 1358, but also used thereafter to refer to any uprising of the peasantry against the landed gentry or establishment.

depicted by Téniers or van Ostade, who so greatly disgusted the great king and outlive his dust – glorified for all that. We don't have a king now, it is true, that such an artist could revolt, but Huysmans, Dutch by race and by the genius of his race, will subsist, like his precursors in painting and for analog reasons, long after the eternal oblivion of the monarchs of journalism, who prepare, once again, to contemn him.

* * *

Ah! it is indeed, it is a proud occasion for them to feel the nausea! Think on it! The rustic lyre lies completely sullied in the dung! There are such chapters, the calving, for example, or better yet, the mating of the bull, both of them executed with a vigor of old etchings, which will plunge all that might still remain of bucolic imaginings into a certain mourning.

Ordinarily, Huysmans is not prodigious with exegesis. Sure of his observation and confident in it, he expects from it alone all possible effect, and he limits himself to presenting it without epilogue. But, having arrived at the so very un-Virgilian bull that he recounts to us and the episode having reached a climax, that profaner of the old ciboria of rhetoric who, after all, did not take a vow of eternal impassiveness, like Flaubert, can no longer contain himself, and here is his commentary:

"Jacques began to believe that there was epic grandeur in the bull as in the golden wheat, an old commonplace, an old Romantic rag patch-worked together by poetasters and novelists of the present era!

No, actually, there was nothing there to get all worked up about, to put on soft leather boots and blow the horn! It was neither impressive, nor lofty. As far as lyricism goes, the mating consisted of a mass of two sorts of flesh that one beat, that one piled on top of one another, that one led away then, as soon as they had copulated, by beating on them again!"

Same thing for the *golden wheat*:

"'What a joke the golden wheat!' he said to himself, looking from afar at those sheaves of a dirty orange color, collected into piles. Try as he might, he could not succeed in finding that that picture of the harvest so constantly celebrated by painters and poets was really great. There were, under an inimitable blue sky, men with their shirts off and hairy chests, stinking of sweat, and who scythed rust-colored copses. My how that painting seemed mean compared to the scene in a factory or the belly of a ship liner, lit up by the fire of the boilers!

"What was the anodyne work of the fields, in sum, compared to the horrible magnificence of machines – that one beauty that the modern world was able to create? What was that golden crop, the facile parturition of a benevolent soil, the painless labor of a land fecundated by the seed escaped from the hands of a brute, in comparison to that birthing from cast iron copulated by men, to those embryos of steel exited from the womb of furnaces, and forming, and pushing, and growing, and crying in raucous plaints, and flying along the rails, and moving mountains, and crushing rocks!

"The nourishing bread of machines, the hard anthracite, the somber coal, all that black harvest mowed down in the entrails even of the soil, in the dark of night, was exceptionally dolorous, exceptionally grand!"

The citations could go on endlessly. But that page, – is it not particularly magnanimous, in brief, for a contemptuous fellow of that breadth?

One would have to stop somewhere, clearly, but how can I refuse to cite this savorous and supreme tidbit for the gourmands of poetry:

"The night, having grown darker, seemed to rise up from the earth, drowning the paths and the massifs, condensing the sparse bush, encircling the vanished trunks of trees, coagulating the twigs of the branches, filling the holes between the mixed-up leaves in a single and unique tuft of darkness; and, compact and dense almost, from below, the night volatilized as it reached the spared tops of the pines.

"Finally, above the church, the garden, the woods, high above, in the hard sky, the cold water was seeping from the stars. One might have said, for the most part, luminous and glacial sources, and as for those that burned more brightly still, inverted geysers, sources of warm light returned. There was not a wave, not a cloud, not a fold in that firmament that would suggest the image of a steady sea scattered with liquid islets.

"Jacques felt that weakness in all his body that the vertigo of eyes lost in space brings on.

"The immensity of that taciturn ocean, with archipelagoes illuminated by feverish flames, left him nearly trembling, overcome by that sensation of a stranger to the emptiness before which the suffocated soul grows alarmed.

"And, behind the chateau, in turn, the moon rose up, full and round, like a gaping well descending to the bottom of the abyss, and bringing back, to the level of its silver coping, pails of pale fire."

* * *

The purely psychological parts of *En Rade* are such that one must, by necessity, refer the reader to them, without spoiling, by the least citation, the sensations he will find there. Certain explorations into the darkness of hearts – into those seething abysses where reside what Huysmans calls "the unconscious ignominy of elevated souls" – will make one's hair stand on end and give shudders of agony as of someone fallen into a crater. The correct abomination of familial manipulations, for example, cannot be denounced in a more exquisitely atrocious fashion, nor by so mockingly executionary a diabolical plume. As I said at the beginning, this book will make you shudder.

Logically, our dog of a century must in this way come to an end, and with cantilenas it must accompany its demise. If, as has so often been announced, terrifying manifestations in the skies, earth--shaking epiphanies, and surpassing massacres must signal the imminent return of a God of justice, hats off to such prophets who haven't even got the need to be conscious of an inspiration in order to vociferate the fall of humankind! Everything is desirable and holy respecting whatever can cast the old world down. One must have had entirely enough of being so disgusting and so cadaverously rotten under impassive constellations!

But if, by inconceivable decree, the Lord God was not supposed to have done anything, and if one ought not to have hoped for any celestial cleansing of the world, the necessity of demolishing everything would appear to be all the more pressing, and the universal need could be let loose finally to rush pell-mell together with filthy souls and cowardly spirits towards the brotherly shithole where the theological hope of Nihilism already ferments!

When books such as the one just discussed at length echo the moral state of an entire world, it is very possible that, although at dawn one had heard harmonious sighs, at evening – there is a howling!

– Fontenay-aux-Roses, 1887.

After Conversion

The Incarnation of the Adverb[14]

Bees sometimes land on excrement.
They seem to find honey there.
— Words of a HORNET

When the first pages of *Là-Bas* appeared, in *Paris Echo*, I was deep within a Scandinavian desert little visited by æsthetic emotions. A faithful friend sent me this novelty however, and a reading of the liminary chapter shook me with such fiery enthusiasm that, without expecting what had to follow, I expedited, forthwith, to the author, a pathetic message. I even promised him to be more eloquent still and to hang his name on the capitals of the sky when his work was definitively published.

I am going to keep my word then today as best I can, but without hoping that des Esseintes' joy will equal my zeal.

In fact, the overall vision of *Là-Bas* scarcely delayed me in delivering myself of my lyrical congestion. I am forced to recognize even, while groaning, in spite of certain curious pages whose *stamp is in-*

---

[14]The Incarnation of the Adverb: first published as "Incarnation de l'adverbe" in *The Plume*, no 51, June 1, 1891. The article was on the front page, and the subsequent three pages after that.

contestable, that Huysmans' new book is the most monstrously futile of contemporary rhapsodies.

I do not believe that literary uncircumcision has yet displayed so furious a dissoluteness of anarchic information.

That book is an extraordinary jumble, a brawl, a scramble, a pell-mell, a cataclysm of *documents*, for the celebrated writer manifests himself more than ever as a cataract out of the documentary sky.

God only knows what a book costs that poor wretch equally incapable of inventing and divining. The entire existence of such a notetaker is evidently devoted to *marginalia* and scratchpads. When the harvest is sufficiently copious, he opens up half-way apropos of – it does not matter what, – and that turns into a book like *Là-Bas*, which I defy the most sagacious of critics to determine the tendency of.

***

In *À Rebours*, the procedure was the same, doubtless, because the author knows no other, but at least he had a kind of central and vertebral idea that could give the illusion of unity.

Ah! it was not staggering in its genius, it did not blind one's eyes by the strength of its brightness, that rag of an idea borrowed from the flea-ridden metaphysics of Schopenhauer: "Alone, the worst comes!" Such was the concept.

Men are pigs, women sows, and society is

nothing but an immense heap of carrion. By consequence, Faith, Hope, Love, Enthusiasm, all the great motivations in Life must be ridiculed and dishonored like the gullible hallucinations of a fifteen-year-old.

Huysmans, at thirty-five years old, imagined then an individual radically cured of virtue, marvelously operated on, in his heart and even in his head, having, by dint of *ecus*, realized the delicate refuge of a princely boutique of æsthetic curiosities.

His mind could enter only backwards into that hermitage because inflexible confinement was the only option, perpetually, between antinomy and its exact opposite. The "sesame" of that place, it was to be *rare,* and to detest the tradition of the human race. I do not know whether so firm a bias has ever been seen before to dismiss Truth and Beauty in order to admit only anomaly and deviation, – even the *exception* being abhorred if it implicated the equilibrium of strength or grandeur.

The future will be surprised by the unprecedented childishness of a popular book wherein the orchids of India – for example – are deemed superior to the most beautiful flowers of the Occident; for this fairly *Dutch* reason that it is difficult to acquire them and that they cost a lot of money!...

It is true that the experiment ended by a salutary disgust. The author, nauseated by the identical drivel of his character, immediately slammed his book shut while letting out a loud cry to God... How in the world could one have guessed that that clamor was yet another literary artifice?

* * *

From that day forward, Huysmans was regarded as a pessimist who was evolving towards Christianity. One could even believe that evolution virtually accomplished in a writer who prided himself on his independence and who need not have, in sum, obeyed anything but his æsthetic faculties. Wasn't it necessary for our epoch of demolition and trembling that such an adventure should become possible?... It was spelled out in very large letters.

A man who was called extraordinary, pushed towards God by despair, by contempt, by the horror of contemporary banality, by all the needs of his artistic soul and, nevertheless, wanting to have nothing to do with that terrible God and debating within himself with rage while caught in his luminous nets! What a scene! The admiration of several naïve people exceeded all conjecture, and the surprise of many shrewd ones was extreme.

Evidently, there was nothing more to expect and, in order to get on with it, numerous elms were planted along the rectilinear road of the Tribunal of Penitence.

Years passed and three new books appeared: *En Rade, A Dilemma, Certains*. In the first, the pessimism of *À Rebours* was simply aggravated in a demoniac way, without compensation of any sort. It was a little discouraging. Nothing so very theological moreover transpired through the other two. The spiritualism of that novelist didn't uncoil itself.

At a pinch, that could be explained by the insufficiency of the occasion, it could very well be explained even by the hair's breadth tenuity of those fantasies that were really foreign to all divine premeditation, and believers got fed up in the inexpugnable will of patiently waiting for an eternity.

In the end, however, *Là-Bas* was announced to be a decisive work. *A Study of Satanism* is what the journal that published it said. Evidently the writer who declared, beforehand, his haughty resolution to rejoice, from then on, "outside of time," went, in earnest, this time, to rush headlong towards heaven, and the first pages of that book were such that one could definitely believe he had already left earth.

* * *

"The conception of *Là-Bas*," I wrote to him, "of course exceeds my conjectures, but what a prodigious debut was that evocation of the *Christ of the Poor*! You are becoming, my dear Huysmans, a passionate Catholic. You are no longer in control of your soul, it is your soul that leads you on, along those admirable paths *into the abyss*, from the literary life to the contemplative life.

"Haven't you clearly expressed yourself already? After *À Rebours* and *En Rade,* you were at the very extreme end of the impasse. You needed to either expire in the cul-de-sac or find another way.

"You remember Nicolardot explaining your

pessimism in terms of your absolute ignorance of 'good places.' We laughed about it several times together, but don't you think, decidedly, that that grotesque was right. You were ignorant of the *good place*. You seem to recognize it today and that explains your superb, renewed talent in an indefectible manner, because you are on the threshold of ecstasy and magnificence."

Eh, well, I chose the wrong adverb. Huysmans had written *Là-Bas* and I stubbornly insisted on reading *Là-Haut*. That explains everything.

One of his pupils, mildly disappointed, expressed the timid wish that the author's vacillating aspirations might henceforth be guaranteed by the decisive choice of that new label. But the mistake of that good disciple is even graver than my own.

The truth is that Huysmans really wanted to write *Là-Haut*, which he *believed* he wrote – and his nature precipitated him into the other Abyss. His gravitation is towards Darkness; his abominable book no longer allows any doubt about it.

Darkness of reason, darkness of heart, darkness about life, and darkness about death, it is horribly complete!

When he says, for example, that "conversations that don't treat of religion or art are vain and low"; when he declares his admiration for the Trappists or the Carthusians, his fondness for the matutinal call of bells, his indignant contempt for mediocre Catholics and priests lacking in fervor, etc.; finally, when he writes gropingly ten obscure pages on the effusion of the Paraclete and the imminent approach of "Christ in glory"; be persuaded that he uses the notes that someone else has given him and that his soul has no share in the illusion of nascent Christianity that that chatter can produce.

Fundamentally, – it is terrible to think about it – Huysmans is the zealot of the nightmares and deformities that he puts on display, and the refined complaisance of his portrayals is the proof of it. Given formal notice to manifest once and for all his predilection, that wan skeptic shut himself up in the "Iron Tower of Hysterias" so as better to outrage the "Nazarene."

* * *

That could still possess a certain infernal grandeur if the boldness of a precise idea was not essentially lacking and, above all, if one did not feel, at each instant, the impersonality of a poor man who is anxious to come out with all his *documents*.

And what a horrifying downpour of so-called information that he had collected from everywhere for years! To think that that book has the pretension of informing us on the symbolism of bells, on the Middle Ages, on the story of Gilles de Rais, on medicine, pharmacy, sadism, vampirism, spiritualism, astrology, theurgy, magic, incubuses, succubuses, bewitchment, and liturgy; and finally on the black mass, on the sacrifice of Melchizedek, on the Antichrist and the Paraclete!

All that without prejudice to the intermediary insights into Naturalism, painting, money, women, priests, cuisine, theology, and, in general, anything that can be the object of human understanding.

The only thing absolutely missing is what I said earlier, a concept that belongs exclusively to the author, a personal and umbilical idea that sheds some light for us on the metaphysical genesis of that overgrown compilation, while revealing to us the concern of the compiler. One has read nearly five hundred pages without anything having been sorted out.

If one absolutely wants to take the last phrase of that book for the explanation, the perplexity is hardly diminished, for one would need to suppose then, – against all likelihood – the terrifying mediocrity of a writer capable of putting together eight or nine volumes on the single theme that the human soul is dead and that nothing remains but "to cross one's arms" while listening to the insipid words of a society that is about to die.

Why then, in that case, speak with respect for prayer? Why the phrases, several hundred times, alas! on the peace of the cloister, on the suavity of religious emotions, on the enviable candor of the humble? Why above all that pathological obsession for an *orthodox* satanism that it is impossible to accept without the most formal adherence to the teachings of Catholicism?

One needs to choose or, at least, to stay silent if one was so sopranicized by skepticism as to no longer have the virility of a choice. No literary Byzantine has the right to make an attempt on souls, and it is an act of criminal childishness to accuse the Church – *while taking it seriously* – when one cannot back up one's accusation by eternal considerations.

* * *

The only excuse for that lamentable writer is the unconsciousness I've spoken about. Huysmans has often expressed his contempt of and hatred for "dilettantism in art," but there is no doubt that he practices religious dilettantism, which is more serious and certainly more devoid of genius, if that is possible.

More than any other person, however, he had been warned. One knows that, for five years, he was close friends with someone among his contemporaries who was best able to orient him. It was an incredible lease of suggestions, demonstrations, exhortations and counsels. The most generous of aliments were conferred with patience on that debile stomach that was incapable of digesting anything.

The only result of that impossible act of rendering the field cultivable was the monstrous journal of undiscerning and incohesive notes from which *Là-Bas* finally emanated. The divulger of the Absolute who suckled him must be mediocrely satisfied with his suckling.

Not only did he not understand anything of the general ideas that one tried to instill in him, but he fragmented and distorted them, like a barbarous schoolkid, while covering his tracks.

His work has thus become an appalling hodgepodge of materials originally destined for the construction of a great book and deteriorated capriciously by the perversity of an impotent man.

One encounters in it, at every instant, the trace of a foreign thought, sometimes even entire blocks inexplicably escaped from the rage of a demolisher and which make one see just what a monument could have been constructed by a more obedient and humbler laborer.

But at first one would have had to accept, I repeat for the third time, a generative concept, a metaphysical substrate whose norm was inflexible, and that didn't square with the cerebral faculties of the dilettante any more than with the instincts of the profaner.

The providential pedagogue to whom the author of *Là-Bas* owes three-quarters of his book would have assuredly rejoiced in the shadows to have suggested to him a masterpiece, but I doubt he would support without indignation the ignominious travesty of his thought.

Not content with reconciling, by filthy blasphemies, the ardent effusions of a person who bared his soul to him, Huysmans, in his twentieth chapter, discovered, *completely unawares*, the means by which paradoxically and repugnantly to ridicule the religious confidences of the most dolorous hope!

That is really too much, I believe, the abuse of the documentary notebook; and I do not know what is more hateful and despicable – the unqualifiable criminal act of having simply published a woman's[15] letters, *which he would have been incapable of inventing*, or the hideous innocence of that imbecilic profanation.

We get to the Adverb now.

Huysmans' passionate predilection for that *part of speech* is strangely and profoundly characteristic.

For those who seek in a writer's works something other than relaxation or a nervous trepidation, the title of a book has the importance of a monstrance of grandeur and vanity.

Whether he like it or not, the author is forced to expose there his *species,* which the reader's ravishment does not always consecrate.

From that point of view, Huysmans' titles are maybe the most astonishing that exist: *En Ménage, À Rebours, En Rade, À vau-l'eau, Là-Bas.* Note well that they are not even adverbs, but adverbial phrases.

The dynamometer of his mind, it is the adverbial phrase. The simple adverb would be still too precise, too male, too dogmatic, and too sharp for a cerebral apparatus incapable of functioning otherwise than in a subjunctive and satellite mode. The thinking of that man has the sad and distant evolution of the planet of calamities.

---

[15]Original footnote: Mme H. M., Péladan's mistress, who in the novel was called Mme. Chantelouve.

The adverb, according to grammar, is an invariable word that *modifies* the verb, adjective, or another adverb by an idea of place, time, circumstance, etc. That dangerous subaltern is the alpha male of phrases. When it issues a command, it means to devour.

The same adverb, according to Saturnian literature, is a crepuscular vocable that is charged with infecundating Affirmation, stumping with graphite the contours of the Word, and favoring with a fog the monstrous couplings of Antimony. It is the benefactor of Nothingness.

That is why Huysmans idolizes so jealously, to the point of simulacrum, the Adverb, which built for him the chapels where the obscene genitive Prepositions or Conjunctions cannot enter unless trembling, but from which the patibulary Interjections are banished with rage.

* * *

One day Émile Zola, whose greasy mind is oiled only by gliding over the surface of things, got it into his head to depict Huysmans.

The ghostly "Souvarine" in *Germinal* is the physical portrait, frightfully true to life, of that virtuoso of fascination. But that is only a *physical* portrait, the only kind Émile is capable of.

Now, the silent and inhuman nihilist of the Voreaux mine shaft is an active specter who gets along quite well himself, in the darkness, and who

After Conversion

does not send others in his stead. He knocks himself out as much as he can, but by exposing his carcass which does not appear to be a precious piece of furniture to him, and he would not take Olympian airs with anyone who might be made to knock himself out for him. He is a desperate man through and through, that man there, who does not disguise his execrations. Finally, he has above all, for lack of cardinal or theological virtues, the intellectual nobility to obey a fixed idea and to espouse all its consequences.

Would you believe that a single word from that fictive individual was enough to determine the insomnia of des Esseintes?

When Souvarine, having accomplished his disembowelment of the scaffolding in the pit, is on the verge of bearing elsewhere the typhoon of his sectarian furies, without lingering over the futile contemplation of the catastrophe that he has put into motion, someone asks him where he is going. It is then that, extending his arm in a vague gesture, he responds simply: "*Là-Bas.*"

That single phrase, that semblance of an adverb, determined the hatching of the semblance of a book so that now we find Huysmans, sheltered by the atheism of his century, able with impunity to realize on the private intelligence of guards the program of immolation that that fanatic in *Germinal* executed on human bodies, at the risk of his own skin.

And, nevertheless, he does not stop abhorring it, this complacent century. One is tempted to ask whether he is really sincere, and whether his grief about not living in the Middle Ages is anything more than the lamentation of a glib talker. It is the story of the orchids. It would have required the century of Pericles then or the fabulous period of the Egyptian dynasties.

That Middle Ages that he laments would have been, I believe, extremely inhospitable to the oscillations and amphibologies of his art. The men of that period were real men, and they didn't blush for love, innocence, or prayer.

They didn't speak hatefully like him: "My fatherland is wherever I feel well," but instead they said, "I feel well wherever my fatherland is," and it is for that reason that they were willing to die in the presence of that Maid of Orleans among the Archangels whom he dares to accuse of having been *baneful* for France (pages 65 and 66).

The enthusiasts who were crucified by fatigue and penitences for Saint Tombeau would have understood very little of being scared witless before the enemy, as is mentioned in *Sac au dos*, and still less, if that is even possible, of the monastic vow's astonishing assimilation to the brothel manager's need for security, he who disciplines vagabond prostitutes ordinarily (p. 16).

That valiant society being in possession of a pure heart, the gaiety of its Blessed didn't scandalize it, because it thought, contrary to the melancholic author of *Là-Bas,* that customary sadness is a sign of turpitude.

To tell the truth, the VERB *alone was worshipped*, – the adverb and the subadverb not having yet, in those ancient times, anything more than a grammatical existence.

I am therefore firmly persuaded that Providence has not committed that unpardonable error of stuffing the soul of a contemporary of the Crusades into the flannel cloth of a contemporary of M. Zola, and I imagine that Huysmans would have lived inconsolably in a world where profaners were so well roasted.

* * *

"And he was justly accused in the end. That was his fault, his own, if all else failed. He lacked appetite, was not really tormented except by the erethism of his brain. He was worn down in body, frayed in soul, inept at loving, tired of tenderness even before he received it, and so disgusted after having endured it! He had a fallow heart and nothing sprouted. What kind of malady was that then: to defile all pleasures in advance because of reflection, to soil every ideal as soon as one attained it! *He was unable any longer to touch anything, without ruining it*. In that poverty of a soul, everything, except art, was no more than a more or less tedious recreation, a more or less vain diversion."

Thus does our author present himself, on page 272.

A sublime Theology declares to us that, soon after death, souls *judge themselves* in the essential clarity that inundates them, that they precipitate themselves spontaneously, with the most frightening freedom, into the abyss that fits them, and that it is in this way that one must conceive of the redoubtable Tribunal of God.

Is he already dead then, that miserable Huysmans, to make us listen to so mournful a sob?

"Inept at loving!" Inept, consequently, at admiration, and never reflecting but his own image in works of art, which he believes to contemplate.

That morose degustator of the unusual and incomparable, confessed to me, one day, that, never, in a novel, would he make someone say: *I love you,* – sacrificing consequently the material exactitude for which Naturalism is glorified to the tenebrous injunction of a Master whom he does not know.

That phrase has a feeling of panic to it, when you think about it.

* * *

But I do not believe that he has written a great deal since then. After *Là-Bas,* he must have exhausted all his notes, like someone who has spent all his blood, and what the devil do you expect him to say when that happens?

Schopenhauer is not infinite, and it is not really a literary destiny to keep trotting out and rehashing eternally the sententious epiphonemae of that very low prig.

The mosaic of words or phrases, however superfine and complicated one might suppose it, does not lead infinitely far either, especially when the mind of a writer has neither vestibule nor partitions.

And then, besides, what is there to profane now? What remains to pollute and ruin? I'm not a prude, but there really is too much filth nowadays, and disgust abounds in that breviary of sacrilegious suggestions that the Middle Ages would have burnt with dirty wood shavings!

When one thinks about the horrid mark that this book will leave on certain minds, it is alarming to tell oneself that the fratricidal author had received from *someone* the electuary of Truth, the elixir of supreme Hope... and that he made a mortal poison out of it instead, so that his sepulchral soul might not be in any peril of joy and his æsthetic of a galley slave might not be remanded!

– Copenhagen, May 14, 1891.

The Expiation of Jocrisse

One presumes that immediately after the death of abbot Boullan,[16] the celebrated mage of Lyon, the faithful of the Church of Carmel,[17] reunited in a kind of conclave, would have designated, with unanimous voice and loud acclamations, M. Joris-Karl Huysmans for his successor.

The author of *Là-Bas* would from then on become the Sovereign Pontiff according to the order of Melchizedek and the only sublunary at hand to celebrate the "Sacrifice of glory."

Despite the financial prostration caused by the crisis of the Panama, notable sums doubtless will flood in for the erection of a sublime temple exclusively allocated for the ceremonies of the new cult, where less esoteric writers will be able to admire, in robes of vermillion cashmere fastened around their waist and white coats cut in the shape of an upside-down cross on their chest, the Grand Priest who was one of their own.

To be perfectly forthcoming, Huysmans "is on a mission from Heaven to break the infectious

---

[16]Boullan: Joseph-Antoine Boullan (1824-1893), the successor to Eugène Vintras, and known as Elijah John the Baptist.

[17]Church of Carmel: otherwise known as the Brothers of Mercy, of which Eugène Vintras, said to be the reincarnation of Elijah, was the grand priest.

schemes of Satan and to preach the coming of the glorious Christ and the divine Paraclete."

That is why I have entitled this section *The Expiation of Jocrisse*.

But all that, in truth, partakes of a deep sadness. I was quite peaceful, my faith! in my little Catholic dungeon, in the process of putting my military memories[18] in order. Someone came to me to ask my advice on the Satanic prattle. Someone paid me the honor of supposing that my feelings about contemporary mages would be expressed efficaciously for the edification or the recoverance of some lost sheep.

I consent then. All the same, I hope to surprise nobody, by declaring, beforehand, that it would be better, *perhaps*, simply to consult with the Pope, unless one preferred to reread carefully the mediocre transcription of the dictionary of heresies that Flaubert entitled *La Tentation de Saint Antoine*.[19]

* * *

That poor Huysmans! He had begun so fortuitously with *The Vatard Sisters* and *À vau-l'eau*. He had gotten off to such a good start. Already even, he succeeded in copying rather tidily Lucien Descaves' honorable adjectives.

Why did he have to encounter that abbot

---

[18]Original footnote: military memories: I was writing *Sueur de Sang* at that time. – L.B.

[19]*La Tentation de Saint Antoine: The Temptation of Saint Anthony*.

Boullan, that so very uncalm doctor Baptiste, whose atrocious religiosity ought to have put him on guard.

In the name of Heaven, what did Vintras[20] come to do, that predecessor of Boullan, that miller's assistant full of apocalypses, in the fated calm of that project plan from the banlieues.

Alas! the miserable wretch had written *À Rebours*. Obsessed by that adverbial locution, he found himself defenseless against a horrible chasuble of carnival wherein the cross was depicted *upside down.*

Little informed on universal history, he must have thought that the diametrical opposite of the Catholic Church, and sacerdotal disobedience or turpitude, were stunning novelties, and he persuaded himself that a Carmel where one reveals that "the Paraclete descends into the genitals" ought by necessity to provide shelter to a plausible God.

The enlightener Vintras having moreover taught that "the act of sexual love is, of all homages, the most agreeable to God," – those gymnastics agreeable to men cannot *not* attract a large number of followers.

Huysmans after having glommed onto that doctrine even more than onto Naturalism, of which he was the champion, thought he had found an outlet to heaven. Incapable of intuition and prodigiously de-

---

[20]Vintras: Eugène Vintras (1807-1875), who believed, sometime after Saint Joseph had appeared to him in 1839, that he was the messiah and prophet of the "reign of the Holy Ghost," or the period known as the "freedom of the children of God."

void of the faculty of synthesis, all eyes and no ears, – ignorant, since then, as far as religious things are concerned, his being of the thickest ignorance – it was inevitable that an ignoble priest's dirty profanations should appear like saintly practices to him.

One has read, in the newspapers, the alarming details of the healings of the womb by "the imposition on the ovaries, of consecrated hosts."

It is by *seeing* such acts that the infortunate contemnor of the school's materialism thought to make a dash for the most transcendent spirituality.

For it is certain, and of unwavering tradition, that a smutty religion is the objective of all those who are disobedient to the supernatural authority of the Vicarage of Jesus Christ. It is what the religious renaissance movement, which has been spoken of for several years now, is reduced to, I'm afraid.

* * *

Note well that it is not the street entertainers, harlequins, or scaramouches[21] of occultism that I am looking at precisely. I single out a sincerely gullible person about whom a great noise is being made recently, an unconscious swallower of the oldest swords of magic, and I would have the right, more than many others assuredly, to cry foul – having been for many years the benevolent well from which the ideas and the essential documents of *Là-Bas* were drawn.

---

[21]scaramouche: a stock, comic or clownish character from the *commedia dell'arte*.

I was not the only one consulted by him, oh! no: documentalists take from all hands. But the very foundation of the book, the signification of supernatural realities that he utterly lacked, – God is witness to my efforts, and my patience, to make it penetrate him, slowly...

I have recounted, in the preceding chapter, that deplorable adventure, the memory of which does not fill me with any pride, I would ask you to believe.

I think even that it is appalling to be mistaken for so long, so completely, about a man, and I continually ask God to forgive my incomparable stupidity.[22]

* * *

Such is the pontiff, such is the actual sorcerer of the magic and central cauldron wherein one sees frothing, for several days, all divergent, newly-born satanisms whose monstrous amalgam is ridiculously called occultism or esoterism.

Whether they should curse him or worship him, he has to be their chief, for they cannot act or live except by his name.

I would have really preferred it if he wasn't called Jocrisse. I would have gotten myself upset for *something* at any rate. What I perceive to be the most satanic thing in those young men is their stupidity and their profound asininity. To give just one striking ex-

---

[22]Original footnote: *Etenim homo pacis maæ, in quo speravi: qui edebat panes meos, magnificavit super me supplantationem.* – Psalms XL, 10.

ample of this, – not one person among them has yet been found, I believe, who has asked himself, at the very least, whether Vintras, the founder of the new Carmes and Johannites, self-ordained priest, condemned to prison for manifest fraud, and editor, from the back of his jail cell, of the apocalyptic *Voix de la Septaine*, had been a simple rascal by any chance. Same observation for the abbot Boullan, inhumanely struck, him also, by our penal laws.

It is remarkable, above all, that this latter man, lawfully ordained into the sacerdocy, and who unhesitatingly left the Church in order to attend to more urgent matters, which was to incarnate the soul of Saint John the Baptist, hadn't inspired in any of his admirers the violent need to vindicate him of treason and apostasy.

But go and ask for a like effort from the men who do not even know what the words Obedience, Priest, Church, or Absolute mean, and who are nonetheless very sure to have regained the wisdom of Solomon or the colossal science of Enoch, Seventh Patriarch before the deluge.

I need to stop here because I have the scant enviable honor, I kid you not, of having discovered the supreme Secret, the great Arcana of magicians, and I do not wish to expose myself by letting out such a treasure.

That misfortune happened to me once already, on May 15, 1891, at a very small review. An imprudence that nearly cost me dearly. If it wasn't for the intervention of Prince Ourousof, having rushed expressly from Moscow to defend me, a spell of ten thousand francs would have been cast on me.

It appears that such is the fairest price to pay for the reputation of an esoteric.

– January 24, 1893.

Appendix

Jules Barbey d'Aurevilly's Review of *À Rebours*[23]

A REBOURS

By J.-K. Huysmans

Our readers will recall the articles that we dedicated to the latest novel by M. J.-K. Huysmans.[24] They will read with interest the very beautiful page of criticism that M. Barbey d'Aurevilly has published on the same subject in Pays, *on July 27. We reproduce it here with a pleasure that is all the greater given we have found in the generous and symphonic prose some ideas that are a little similar to our own.*

Nothing is more honorable for a critic than similar encounters with one of the loftiest literary minds of contemporary France.

---

[23] Jules Barbey d'Aurevilly published an article on *À Rebours,* in the July 28, 1884 issue of *le Constitutionnel*, cited by Huysmans himself in the 1903 preface to that book. It was reprinted in the August 17, 1884 issue of the Belgian journal *L'Art Moderne*, on which this is based.

[24] Original footnote: See the July 13 and 20, 1884 issues of *L'Art Moderne*.

I

À rebours! Going backwards! Yes! going backwards in the common sense, in the moral sense, from reason, from nature, such is this book that cuts like a razor, – but a poisoned razor – on the inept and impious platitudes of contemporary literature. Of talent however, alas! it has some, and more than one could wish for and more than one could have believed, coming from the author of this book, already known for works of a much inferior tone to this one. Until now, M. J.-K. Huysmans has been content to stumble along behind M. Zola, the goat of the literary flock that goes around grazing, in the novel, on the wild thyme of the lowest realities. He was what they call "a Naturalist." Poorly chosen word, that their pretension imposed, even on those who do not accept their pretension. M. J.-K. Huysmans, the author of *The Vatard Sisters*, seemed destined to remain among the soulless photographers lacking in ideas who make up that school, at the present hour, but it appears that he had more soul than the rest of the group, and with this he distances himself from them today. The schism is threatening, it is not complete. M. J.-K. Huysmans has not, himself, the greasy optimism of M. Zola! He does not have, himself, the *joie de vivre!* although he might want it also like nobody else! And it is precisely because he does not have it that he wants to turn everything inside out!

It's insane, – but it's desperate! It's more then than the photographers of literature can give! The latest book by M. J.-K. Huysmans, for whom life is not the pasture of Zola, is then, at bottom, the book of a desperate man, and its title would not suggest half its scope, if the author had not underlined it with an epigraph that surprises and perhaps warns... Would one believe it? the author took it from one of the greatest mystics of the XIVth century! Now, the Naturalists of our age are not mystics. They must even, I imagine, do the mystics a great honor by contemning them. Those kinds of people hardly read Ludolphe and Tauler, and that M. J.-K. Huysmans should put Rusbrock on the cover of his novel, it has got to be that modern Naturalism is cracking apart furiously inside him and that he is beginning to have had enough of that sort of literature in vogue and in which he has set on edge the faculties that would be higher than it... *À rebours* is the story of a soul in pain who recounts his powerlessness to live, even when going backwards! It is the state of a soul that M. J.-K. Huysmans rediscovered and that he has depicted in a book of almost monstrous originality, but which, certainly, is not a paradox, – a new way of beating at cards, in the novel, in order to add life back into the game, – so common and so cruelly boring today.

Evidently there is more to it than that. M. Huysmans' hero, – and the heroes of novels that we write are always a bit like ourselves – is a sick man like all the heroes in the novels of this sick epoch. He is prey to the neuroses of the century. He is a patient of Charcot hospital. A novel's hero who is sound in mind and body and who acts with all his faculties in their perfect equilibrium is an infinitely rare thing and almost a phenomenon. Previously, the phenomenon existed. The passion that makes novels disturbed that equilibrium and alienated man's freedom, but it did not suppress it. At present, it has been suppressed. Of all the freedoms that one puts on an external appearance to believe in, it is the freedom of the soul that one believes in the least. Now, before becoming passionate, one is ill... One has even invented illnesses from before birth, which does not annoy me, me who am a Christian, and who believe in original sin, but which ought to make others at least reflect, who deny it... That is called atavism and presently is making the rounds in literature. M. Huysmans' hero has ancestors from the time of Henri III, and that's the explanation of one of his vices... For those of us who speak another language than all that scientific slang, M. Huysmans' neuropath is a soul sick for the infinite in a society that no longer believes in anything but finite things. Having pushed himself to the the point where his sensations cannot take any more, but still hungry for more sensations, he thinks about taking his life backwards, it's the only thing left for him in order to find some pleasure or some taste, and he takes it, that course of action of a life in reverse, and he describes all the vain efforts he makes to do so. Only, I'm not quite so sure of it, but whatever the case I believe he doubts it... While writing the autobiography of his hero, he is actually writing the particular confession of a depraved and solitary personality, but at the same time he writes, for us, the nosography of a society putrified by materialism, and that gives to his book a unique importance that other psychological novels of this period do not possess.

II

For psychology, which permeates everything, permeates the novel too. Ever since the glorious Balzac, – who believed in God and even the Church, – and who introduced that psychology into his own, but in the right measure of its existence, it grew immensely like the materialism of which it is the daughter. True, we are no longer at the point of La Mettrie's *plant man* or Helvetius' animal hand. We no longer say with the coarse brutality of Cabanis: "Thought in man is nothing but an excrement of his brain"; but we say philosophically and exactly the same thing, using different words and another style. For us, the spinal chord and nerves are what we use to explain the entire man. Des Esseintes (the poor wretch whose story M. Huysmans told) is subject, over the entire coarse of the novel, to that terrible fatality of nerves, stronger than his will or his masters. Des Esseintes is no longer an organism in the manner of *Obermann, René, Adolphe*, – those heroes of human novels, passionate and culpable. It's a mechanism gone wrong. Nothing more. The interest in that malfunctioning would be mediocre if that mechanism didn't suffer for it, if that singular clock, which was not made in a vacuum and which tries to get its act together and control itself, didn't contain in itself something stronger than itself that prevents it from doing so and tortures it... And, alone, without that torture the novel would cease to exist! It would be nothing more than a dreadful book, puerile and perverse; but that torture, that irremediable torture, avenges us of its perversity!

Without it, one would not reach the end. It would fall out of one's hands. The bibelot collectors of this decadent epoch, the so-called refined sort, those artificial fellows, inanely taken in by all the chinoiserie of material civilisations, those perverted by *ennui* for whom the simple beauty of things no longer suffices, would be the only people to read it. They alone, those blasé sorts, fallen into the infancy of old civilisations, would take an interest in the efforts and retorsions of that miserable Des Esseintes, corrupted by ennui, which engenders all the other corruptions and who imagines that one can go backwards in life, – this difficulty of a life! – as easily as one moves his bibelots from one shelf to another! They alone, those sick and tired, would recognise the ragout maybe in the destructive childishness of that inverted household, for the flaw in M. Huysmans' book, as horrible as that book might be, is not only, as I have said, its being appalling in its philosophy, but it is its puerility in art. In art, there is better to offer us and to make us admire. Des Esseintes is rich. With the money he has, all his fantasies can be played out, and they can be grandiose. Eh, well, except for two or three places in the novel where Des Esseintes is content with being completely abominable, – for example, when he pays two or three months' rent for a very young man to visit the brothel, only later to find enjoyment in turning him into an assassin – the rest of the time, the means he employs to escape the vulgarities of life are pitiful. When he isn't a blackguard, he is a wimp... He makes idiotic and ridiculous inventions. Recall the story of the tortoise whose shell he pays to have gilded and in which he has embedded precious stones! Do you recall the books in his library whose bindings are supposed to reflect their contents? Recall the paper flowers that are supposed to ape natural flowers! Recall the alchemy of his perfumes, crazily sought after for their combinations of unknown scents! and tell me if such poor imaginations are worth the effort of being so absurd! Assuredly, I understand quite well that the vulgarities of life repugn an elevated and proud mind, but, to try to escape them and replace them, one does not have to fall into a small infinity of petty things... Now, M. Huysmans' Des Esseintes, who acts the Titan against life, shows himself to be nothing but an imbecilic Tom Thumb, when he tries to change it!

III

And therein lies the punishment of such a book, one of the most decadent that we could count among the decadent books of this century of decadence. It is not at all, for all that, because of its talent that it is decadent, it is by its use of that talent. The talent, in fact, is evident on every page. The abundance of notions on all things is profuse. The style, demonstrating scholarship and technique, deploys a magnificent richness of vocables that resemble the precious stones embedded into the tortoise shell, and which make it die finally. That superb style however will not save the unprecedented book in which it shines. Exceptionally depraved, M. Huysmans' autobiographical hero loves all things decadent in literature. By choice and by reflection, he prefers, for example, the barbarous

Latin of the Middle Ages to the Latin of the period of Augustus, and places Lucian above Virgil whom he would dishonor with his criticism, as if a genius like Virgil could ever be dishonored! Clearly, that a decadent of that force could be produced and a book like Huysmans' could sprout in a human brain, it really was necessary that we should become what we are – a race at its last hour! A human brain, as genial and as disturbed as it might be, matters little to humanity. It does not count in the human pile. One can pass by it and be quiet, and even not notice it. But when that brain is the expression of an entire society and is equated with it, then it matters and is worthy of the moralist's and the historian's cry, and we are expressing that today!

Never has a more formidable account been given previously on a reasonable and rhythmical society, but which, in the last few years, so much good sense has caused to stumble. Never has the extravagance of a book more energetically given testimony of universal extravagance. History has had other decadences than our own. Societies that come to an end, lost nations, races on the verge of dying, all leave behind themselves precursors of their agony. Rome and Byzantium had theirs, but I do not believe one has found in their ruins a book like this one. Procopius and Petronius are merely historians that recount, to be honest, shameful and lamentable things. But they don't touch life – the essence of life – they don't go after it relentlessly and fiercely. They do not affirm that the world made by God is to be remade. They are not at all reformers against God! They don't have the splenetic audacity of a simple novelist of the XIXth century who believes he's able to create a life that runs counter to life. M. J.-K. Huysmans' book is also not a history of the decadence of a society, but of the decadence of integral humanity. His book is more byzantine than Byzance even. The theologaster Byzance believed in God, because she discussed his Trinity, and she did not have the perverted pride to want to redo the creation of that God as she thought fit. That old and inept lover of histrions and coach drivers demeaned and debased herself in the small things in which people who were great die, and who, when they are old, bend down as low as the ground, but she didn't lower herself to things so small as the things invented by a novelist bored with the work of God!

IV

And that would really be insupportable if there was not at the bottom of that ennui and of all those impotent efforts to deceive it, a bit of grief that does more to elevate the book than its talent even. Undertaken in despair, he touches on, when he finishes, a despair that is greater than the one he began with. At the end of all the incredible madness that he dares, the author felt the deep distress of deception. A mortal anguish is released from this book. The miserable house of cards – that little Babel made of paper – raised against God's world has caved in and collapsed in his hands. The materialist who demanded everything from matter was able to draw from it only what it can give, and that insufficiently. The rebel felt his nothingness. Expiatory thing of the criminal aberrations of this book! The last words are a prayer. It's to a prayer that all that torrent of imprecations and enraged maledictions leads. "'Ah!' he said, 'courage fails me and my heart lifts me... Lord! have pity on the Christian who doubts, on the unbeliever who would believe, on the convict for life who embarks in the night under a firmament that the consoling beacons of hope no longer illuminate!'" Isn't that rather humble and submissive?... It is more so than the prayer by Baudelaire:

> *Ah! Lord, give me the strength and courage*
> *To contemplate my body and heart without*
> *[disgust!*

Baudelaire, the satanic Baudelaire, who died a Christian, has to be one of M. Huysmans' admirations. One feels his presence, like a source of heat, behind the most beautiful pages that M. Huysmans wrote. Eh, well! one day, I challenged the originality of Baudelaire to rewrite *The Flowers of Evil,* but to take it one step further in the worn-out direction of blasphemy. Today, I would be quite capable of challenging similarly the author of *À rebours*: "After *The Flowers of Evil,*" I said to Baudelaire, "you have no other choice, logically, – either the end of a pistol or the foot of the cross." Baudelaire chose the foot of the cross.

But what will the author of *À rebours* choose?

Other Books by the Publisher

Fanchette's Pretty Little Foot
by Restif de La Bretonne,
translated by Richard Robinson

Je M'Accuse...
by Léon Bloy,
translated by Richard Robinson

My Hospitals & My Prisons
by Paul Verlaine,
translated by Richard Robinson

Salvation Through the Jews
by Léon Bloy,
translated by Richard Robinson

Words of a Demolitions Contractor
by Léon Bloy,
translated by Richard Robinson

Cellulely
by Paul Verlaine,
translated by Richard Robinson

Flowers of Bitumen
by Émile Goudeau,
translated by Richard Robinson

Songs for Her & Odes in Her Honor
by Paul Verlaine,
translated by Richard Robinson

www.ingramcontent.com/pod-product-compliance
Lightning Source LLC
Chambersburg PA
CBHW030535080526
44585CB00014B/951